Behind The Wheel™

Denny Hamlin

NASCAR Driver

Sarah Sawyer

rosen publishing's
rosen central®

New York

Published in 2009 by The Rosen Publishing Group, Inc.
29 East 21st Street, New York, NY 10010

Copyright © 2009 by The Rosen Publishing Group, Inc.

First Edition

Library of Congress Cataloging-in-Publication Data

Sawyer, Sarah.
Denny Hamlin: NASCAR driver / Sarah Sawyer.—1st ed.
      p. cm.—(Behind the wheel)
Includes bibliographical references and index.
ISBN-13: 978-1-4042-1895-6 (library binding)
ISBN-13: 978-1-4358-5402-4 (pbk)
ISBN-13: 978-1-4358-5408-6 (6 pack)
1. Hamlin, Denny, 1980– —Juvenile literature. 2. Stock car drivers—
United States—Biography—Juvenile literature. I. Title.
GV1032.H24S39 2009
796.72092—dc22
[B]

                                                                  2008020449

Manufactured in the United States of America

On the cover: Denny Hamlin, driver of the #11 FedEx Freight Chevrolet, sits in his car in the garage area prior to practice for the NASCAR Nextel Cup Series Sharpie 500 at Bristol Motor Speedway on August 24, 2007, in Bristol, Tennessee.

CONTENTS

Introduction 4

Chapter **1** Denny's Early Years 8

Chapter **2** Moving to the Front of the Pack 17

Chapter **3** NASCAR Speed Racer 24

Chapter **4** A Change of Fortune 30

Chapter **5** Paying It Forward 36

Glossary 41

For More Information 42

For Further Reading 44

Bibliography 45

Index 47

Introduction

It was 389 laps before Denny Hamlin thought he really had a chance at the Sprint Cup on March 30, 2008, during the Goody's Cool Orange 500 in Martinsville, Virginia. Jeff Gordon, winner of eight consecutive Sprint Cups, entered pit road on lap 389 just like the rest of the front-runners, including Hamlin. While other lead drivers fueled up and had fresh tires put on their cars, Hamlin opted just for gas. In this way, he was able to cut his pit stop time short and throttle his #11 car out of the pits ahead of everyone else. Everyone, that is, except Jeff Burton. Burton skipped the pit stop altogether.

Burton's strategy didn't keep Hamlin from victory, however. He was on Burton's bumper with 75 laps left in the race. Hamlin moved inside to take the lead. Within two laps, he had passed Burton to take the lead for

Denny Hamlin crosses the finish line ahead of Jeff Gordon to win the 2008 Goody's Cool Orange 500 at Martinsville Speedway in Martinsville, Virginia.

good. Denny Hamlin won the race by 0.398 seconds. Skillful driving and winning strategy took the day! When Hamlin talked to the reporters in Victory Lane, he said, "First Virginia win for me, finally. The curse is over, I think. I hope. We've had such bad luck over these first few weeks."

It was a big win for #11. But even after a major victory, Hamlin couldn't forget that races don't always go this smoothly. He told the Associated Press, "It's just been so close so many times, and to finally break through here, it definitely means a lot. It feels like maybe the monkey is off our back." "Monkey on my back" is a phrase that people use when they have had a streak of bad luck or an ongoing inability to achieve something or attain victory over something. It's a way of saying that something is nagging at you or weighing on you. That is how Hamlin felt before his big win at the Goody's Cool Orange 500.

Hamlin is a great driver. There's no doubt about it. In 79 career Sprint Cup starts, he's enjoyed three amazing wins, five poles, and top-ten finishes in more than half of his starts. But one of the most amazing things to know about him is that he has recorded only two Did Not Finishes (DNFs). This statistic shows that he has amazing knowledge of and respect for his equipment and the sport of racing. He knows how to both drive fast and do it smartly and carefully. He knows how to take chances on the track while ensuring that his car continues to operate smoothly and safely.

But even a great and knowledgeable driver like #11 experiences challenges. Three weeks before this race, his steering went out, ruining his chances for a win. Later, at a race in Bristol, Tennessee, a fuel pickup problem sent him from first to sixth place in almost no time. That's the exciting part of racing—no matter how talented a driver is, any number of things can keep him or her from victory. There's just no way to know what the other drivers will do. That's the magic of racing, and that's why people watch it so avidly. It is also the very same magic that has infused Denny Hamlin's life and racing career.

CHAPTER 1

Denny's Early Years

James Dennis Alan Hamlin Jr. was born on November 18, 1980, in Tampa, Florida. Before his legs were even long enough to reach the pedals, he sat on his father's lap and watched NASCAR Cup races on television. His father says that even then he was able to tell you the name of every driver and the driver's sponsor. During commercial breaks, Hamlin would race two Matchbox cars. According to his dad, he always pretended that one of the cars belonged to Bill Elliott. His mother told Dan Newton of NASCAR.com, "We'd ask him what he wanted to be when he grew up, and he always would say, 'I'm gonna be a racecar driver.' That's been his only focus his entire life."

Hamlin was serious about being a racer. In fact, he began racing even before he had his license. Like many NASCAR drivers, he got his start racing

Hamlin and his mother *(left)* and father *(third from the right)* wait to hear qualifying results at the International Raceway in Richmond, Virginia.

go-karts, or karts. That's when his grandmother, Thelma Clark, knew he'd be a star. Newton quotes her as saying, "Oh golly, I've been following him since he was a little kid. Ever since they built these little cars [go-karts] for him to race around in, he's been winning races." To which Hamlin replied with a smile, "She's got a lot of faith in me, that's for sure!"

Karting

Kids can start go-kart classes at the age of five with "kid karts." At the age of seven or eight, they graduate to karts. These aren't motor-less soapbox derby carts—they are steel machines with motors much like those found in a motorcycle. They're an inexpensive and relatively safe way to get the feel of driving—and the skills needed to race—long before a driver is old enough for a license.

Karting is frequently how young people prepare for a serious racing career. It prepares them for a future in high-speed, wheel-to-wheel racing by helping them develop reflexes, car control, and strategic thinking. In learning the variables that affect the competitiveness of the kart (tire pressure, gearing, seat position, chassis stiffness, etc.), young drivers are learning about the same components that make a great racing car.

Denny Hamlin took advantage of this learning experience. He worked on and drove carts at a very early age, and his talent was recognized even then. At 12, he was a major player in the Junior Restricted League, racing go-karts and winning titles like the Amelia Motor Raceway Track Champion (Junior Restricted), the Virginia Dirt Karting Association State Champion (Junior Champ), and the World Karting Association Virginia Dirt Series State Champion (Junior Champ).

Kart racing is the perfect training ground for future NASCAR drivers.
Denny Hamlin is a former kart champion.

At 15, he'd already been racing go-karts for eight years, with 127 feature wins and five championships in three classes.

Hamlin describes this phase of his career in *Stock Car Racing* magazine: "I'm kind of like a lot of other guys in racing who got started on go-karts when I was seven years old and won a bunch of races." He says, "I actually won my first race, and that led to the next week and the week after that. That's what really got the ball rolling for me. We ended up winning a couple of Virginia state [karting] championships and 186 feature wins before I got into a stock car when I turned 16 years old."

KNOW YOUR KARTS

According to *National Kart News*, there are three common types of karts. Fun karts are the type that you can find at places like K-Mart. They are designed to have fun around your yard and are usually priced around $500. They're designed mainly for kids. Concession karts are those that are used at amusement parks that also offer things like miniature golf and batting cages. You can't buy concession karts in a store. Racing carts are custom-built machines designed to allow you the opportunity to tune and modify them to suit your driving and racing needs and preferences. They are built from the most high-tech, high-performance materials available today. They are too fast for amusement park–style tracks and are built specifically for racing tracks. They are to be driven only by serious and experienced kart racers.

Some drivers love karts so much that they race karts even after they're old enough to get a driver's license and drive a race car. Hamlin was not one of those racers. Even though he did very well racing karts, he couldn't wait to get a license and get into a car.

Racing Karts

Racing karts are custom-built to suit the type of racetrack and race that drivers are most interested in. The three most common track designs and types of kart races are sprint, oval, and enduro.

Sprint

This is the most common and popular type of kart racing. These races are on tracks that resemble real roads. The tracks are generally half a mile (0.80 kilometers) in length. The karts vary in engine size and can drive at somewhere between 45 and 80 miles per hour (72 and 129 km/hr). Most races are short and quick, lasting only about 10–15 laps. This is why they're called "sprint." A sprint is a quick race focused more on speed than on ability to go long distances. Karts used in sprint racing generally cost between $2,000 and $5,000. They can be custom-built for each racer.

Oval

Oval racing occurs on an oval-shaped track surfaced with either asphalt or dirt. Tracks vary widely in length and can be as short as 1/8 mile (201 meters) or as long as ten miles (16 km). Oval racing is less popular than sprint racing but is still quite a draw for young drivers and spectators alike. It is most popular in the Southern regions of the United States, where NASCAR racing is wildly popular, but it can also be found in other regions as well.

You can use a sprint kart to compete in oval racing, but some drivers create karts especially for the oval track. These karts have a chassis—the frame, wheels, and mechanics of the kart—that is engineered just for tight courses with sharp curves upon which the driver only expects to turn in one direction. This makes them unsuitable for road courses, where a driver might turn in multiple directions and on wider curves.

Enduro

"Enduro" is short for "endurance," which is the ability to go for long periods of time over greater distances. If you want to race a kart on world-famous tracks like the Daytona International Speedway, Mid-Ohio, Elkhart Lake, or Road Atlanta, this is the division in which you need to race. But you'll need a very different kind of kart. These karts are very different in design from oval or sprint karts and are built for greater aerodynamic advantage. This means the car uses its shape to slice through air and go faster. Enduro karts are built so that the driver is laying down, rather than sitting up, as in a typical racecar or kart.

A Family Affair

In 1997, Hamlin turned 16, old enough to get a driver's license in the state of Florida. The very day he got his license, he began his first season driving a mini stock car. He quickly became the youngest driver to win a NASCAR mini stock track championship at Langley Speedway. He was even the NASCAR Mini Stock Rookie of the Year for 1997. He broke, and still holds, the NASCAR mini stock track record at Langley Speedway, with a time of 18.025.

According to Dan Newton of NASCAR.com, that's when people started to sense that Hamlin would be a star. Even his grandmother, Thelma Clark, knew it. She was so sure of it that she wrote this letter to four-time Winston Cup champion Jeff Gordon:

Dear Mr. Gordon,

I am an 80-year-old grandmother who has a 16-year-old grandson hopefully following in your racing skills. He has been go-kart racing since he was seven years old (like you), and at the last count he had 130 trophies. He lives in Richmond, VA., and, according to sports people there, he is making a name for himself. Maybe some day you two will race together. Remember the name Denny Hamlin.

Thelma Clark

His grandmother sent this letter off and still carries a copy of it in her purse in case she meets Gordon and gets to say, "I told you so."

Hamlin's grandmother isn't the only one who believed in him. Dan Newton reports that Hamlin's parents, Dennis and Mary Lou, believed enough to sacrifice almost everything to make sure their son could stay in racing. Racing is expensive. Paying for the lessons, equipment, racing fees, car maintenance, and all the other things it takes to stay in the game is quite a financial burden. The Hamlins weren't rich. In order to pay for all the things their son's career required, they took out additional mortgages on their home twice, withdrew all the money in their retirement fund, and sold their valuable collector cars—including a red 1967 Rally Sport convertible Corvette that belonged to Mary Lou.

This was a big and risky investment for the whole family. But it's one they were willing to make. Mary Lou explained it to NASCAR.com, saying, "We knew we were taking a chance. The way that we looked at it, the only ones who would have to suffer the consequences was his Dad and I." She says that, at the time, they weren't sure it would pay off, but they believed in their son and wanted to make sure that they'd be able to say they did everything they could for him.

CHAPTER 2

Moving to the Front of the Pack

Denny Hamlin moves quickly to the head of the pack. This is true when he races, and it was true when he entered racing. Hamlin began racing stock cars at age 16. In his first stock car race at Langley Speedway—the legendary NASCAR track in Virginia—Hamlin took the pole position and won! "I used to go see him in the late-model cars," his grandmother told NASCAR.com. "He would start out on the pole position and lead all the way around. I started feeling sorry for the other people who watch these races because he made them boring."

Hamlin wasn't bored with his success, however. He felt great, and people began to notice him. No longer was he just a kid with promise— he was now a full-fledged racer with serious potential. People wanted to back this winner with sponsorships— and they did.

Hamlin seizes the lead at the NASCAR Sprint Cup Series' Crown Royal Presents the Dan Lowry 400 at Richmond International Raceway.

Dean Motorsports

If you watch NASCAR at all, you know that racers have sponsors. These are companies that support a racer by paying his or her salary and providing equipment. Remember, Hamlin's parents were supporting his career by mortgaging their house and spending their retirement money. Eventually, that money would run out. When it did, Hamlin was planning to give up racing and go home to work in a trailer-hitch business his dad started. But he wasn't quite ready to give up yet. Hamlin needed a backer, and he got one in Dean Motorsports.

Jim Dean, of Dean Motorsports, had been watching Hamlin win for some time and liked what he saw. In 2002, he heard the Hamlins were out of money and ready to call it quits. He decided to get involved. Dean watched Hamlin race at Myrtle Beach, South Carolina. Hamlin won the pole, finished second, and convinced Dean that he was definitely worth backing. "He won only ten races before he went to work for me," Dean told NASCAR.com. "Nobody knew how good he was. Once he got in my equipment, he won 40 races over two years. That's phenomenal. You won't see that on this level too often."

Hamlin continued to win races and quickly rocketed to stardom. It was amazing for him and for the family that supported him. "It still doesn't seem real when we see him on TV and racing with everybody," his mom told NASCAR.com at the time. "It will probably hit us after the next couple of weeks, and things slow down, and we have time to think about it. It's just a dream come true."

It was a dream come true, but one that was about to get even better. Before any of the Hamlins really knew what hit them, Denny was suddenly racing NASCAR!

NASCAR Rulebook

There is a NASCAR rulebook, but unless you are a driver or otherwise working for the organization, you can't get a copy. It is top secret. The rulebook is updated every year and deals mostly with regulations about the ways cars

WHAT IS NASCAR?

A lot of people use the word "NASCAR" to refer to stock car racing in general. NASCAR is a form of stock car racing, but it's also a specific brand and type of racing.

NASCAR is an acronym that stands for the National Association for Stock Car Auto Racing. NASCAR is an organization that oversees many kinds of auto races, including the Sprint Cup Series (formerly known as the Winston Cup and then the Nextel Cup), the Nationwide Series (formerly known as the Busch Series; it is similar to the Sprint Cup Series but has a shorter season and less prize money), and the Craftsman Truck Series (featuring modified racing pickup trucks). NASCAR drivers often race in all three series, but the Sprint Cup Series is what most people associate with NASCAR.

can be built and legal disclaimers stating that racers are driving at their own risk and NASCAR is not responsible for their safety. This is necessary to protect NASCAR, as an organization, from getting sued by drivers who are injured in crashes.

The rulebook ensures that races don't degenerate into a free-for-all. There are rules and points, and to win at NASCAR, or just to be a well-informed fan, you'll need to know what they are.

How NASCAR Races Are Scored

Drivers win races, of course. But their ultimate goal, at least in terms of the Sprint Cup Series, is to win the Sprint Cup. Drivers win the Cup not by winning any one race but by gaining the highest point total throughout the entire season-long series of races.

Over the course of a racing year's series of races, drivers win points. The higher you finish, the more points you win. So, a first-place finisher will win 185 points, while a 43rd place finisher will win 34 points. Points are also won for leading in individual laps and for the person who leads the most laps. The point system allows consistently solid drivers to win the championships. It is often the case that a driver who hasn't won a race all season will nevertheless capture the Sprint Cup.

The "Chase for the Sprint Cup" is the term used to refer to the last ten races of the season during which only the drivers with the most points are allowed to continue racing for the Cup. It is the NASCAR equivalent to baseball's World Series. The season's previous point tallies are wiped clean, and all drivers start again on equal footing. By the end of these ten races, a champion emerges. It's very exciting for fans and for drivers like Hamlin.

Joining a New Team

It wasn't long after Hamlin had been picked up by Dean Motorsports that he was swept off by an even more prominent sponsor with more connections in the sports world. J. D. Gibbs is the son of former NFL head coach and longtime NASCAR team owner Joe Gibbs. A former NASCAR driver himself, J. D. had retired from racing and become president of Joe Gibbs Racing. He met Hamlin through Jim Dean, recognized his talent, and immediately signed him up, although they had no place on the team in which to insert him for almost a whole year. Hamlin's mother told NASCAR.com, "Denny would call them up once a month and say, 'Hey, I'm still here. Do you want to do anything with me?' They would say, 'Sit tight, and we'll be in contact with you.' It must have driven him crazy."

Finally, in 2004, Joe Gibbs Racing sent Hamlin to run his first Truck Series race at O'Reilly Raceway Park. He finished in tenth place. That same year, he finished eighth in the Busch Series race at Darlington Raceway. With every race he drove, more and more people would start to realize that Hamlin had something special. His new boss was impressed. Hamlin had a bright future ahead of him with Joe Gibbs Racing.

Denny Hamlin talks things over with Joe Gibbs *(left)* at the Talladega Superspeedway in Alabama.

In 2005, Hamlin raced the full Busch Series (now known as the Nationwide Series) season sponsored by Rockwell Automation Chevrolet. He finished fifth in the final points tally, making quite a splash as a rookie. He finished in the top ten 11 times and earned $1,064,110. His parents' financial sacrifices were finally paying off.

Hamlin also raced in the Nextel Cup Series (now known as the Sprint Cup) at the Kansas Speedway, driving a #11 Chevrolet sponsored by FedEx. He drove in seven races, picking up after Jason Leffler was let go, and he made three top-ten finishes and one pole. It was an amazing year, one that proved he was ready for his first full season racing the NASCAR Nextel Cup Series.

NASCAR Speed Racer

Hamlin raced his first full NASCAR Nextel Cup Series season in 2006. He also drove in the Busch Series. This was the big leagues. It was time for Hamlin to make the leap from being a promising rookie to being a genuine contender among the biggest names in racing.

A Fast Start, a Careless Accident

To begin the season, he took part in his first restrictor plate race in the Nextel Cup Series Budweiser Shootout at the Daytona International Speedway. A restrictor plate is a device installed at the engine intake, limiting its turbo power and thus making for a safer, slower, and more competitive race. With seemingly little effort, he beat all the previous year's pole winners in the 70-lap race. He was the first NASCAR rookie to ever do this.

Hamlin burns out his #20 Rockwell Automation Chevrolet, his way of celebrating a win at the 2007 NASCAR Busch Series Diamond Hill Plywood 200.

People took notice. On March 5, he took his first Busch Series victory at Autodromo Hermanos Rodriguez, in Mexico City, and scored a second soon thereafter at Darlington Raceway, in Darlington, North Carolina, in the Diamond Hill Plywood 200.

Hamlin was scoring big points and having big fun. For such a young and relatively inexperienced driver, he was staying remarkably loose. During a break from testing at Lowe's Motor Speedway, he was goofing off with his crew members, racing around his trailer and timing himself. This kind of lighthearted fun wasn't surprising. Those who know Hamlin refer to him often as a big kid. Yet, sometimes this playfulness revealed an immaturity that could lead to trouble. In fact, Hamlin seriously hurt his left hand below the pinky and above the wrist.

The NASCAR radio show "The Final Lap" with Kerry Murphey quotes Hamlin as saying, "The guys were having races around the hauler after the test. I thought I'd try for the best lap of the night, and as I was running around the front of the truck, I caught my hand on a sharp piece of chrome. I got all stitched up, and I'll be fine to race this weekend. By the way, I did finish first [in the trailer race with his crew]. Hopefully Coach Gibbs will be impressed that I can play 'hurt.'" Play hurt he did. Though he had to get 19 stitches and was bandaged up, Hamlin still managed to race and finish second at the Crown Royal 400, losing to none other than NASCAR legend Dale Earnhardt Jr.

Good Luck and a Great Pit Crew

One month later, the Pocono 500 brought Hamlin his first career Cup win and second career pole. It was an unbelievable win. Chris "Spider" Gillin, car chief for Hamlin, described the victory to NASCAR.com, saying, "I still can't believe we finished, let alone won the race. It was a miracle!" Hamlin had blown a tire on lap 51 and spun through grass, but that was only one of the reasons he shouldn't have won the race.

A blown tire and a crash can mean the end of a car, especially when it's driven under stressful and incredibly fast conditions like a NASCAR race. But Hamlin's pit crew was shocked to find that the car's suspension wasn't damaged at all, the brake line was intact, and the car was able to limp to the pit road for repair. NASCAR.com describes the combination of luck and pit crew skill that kept Hamlin in the race: "It took eight pit stops just to patch the car back up. The team got another tremendous break when the yellow flag flew twice just after Hamlin's crash, giving the team the time it needed to fix everything." Spider continued, "Our initial reaction was, 'Our day is over.' Once we went back to the green flag, Denny said, 'This thing isn't so bad. I am still passing cars.'"

Hamlin takes a pit stop at the Nextel Cup Series Pocono 500. It takes a crew of expert mechanics and technicians to keep him on the track and racing to win.

By lap 73, Hamlin saw that his car still had "zip," and by lap 132, he was back in the lead and stayed there throughout the rest of the race. It just goes to show, you never quite know what will happen on the track.

Hamlin's good luck held out. He didn't even have to wait a month for his next career win. Winning the

Pennsylvania 500, also held at the Pocono Raceway, made him only the second rookie in Nextel Cup history to win both the Pennsylvania 500 and the Pocono 500 on the same track during the same season from the pole position.

It seemed like nothing could go wrong for Hamlin, and his winning year was rewarded. In 2006, he won the Raybestos Rookie of the Year award and finished third in the final Nextel Cup standings. He boasted the highest scoring for a NASCAR rookie and the first one ever to chase for the Nextel Cup. Most drivers dream of racing in the big time. But few dream of chasing the Cup their first year out. Yet, that's exactly what #11 did.

CHAPTER 4

A Change of Fortune

The following year, 2007, brought a change of luck for Denny Hamlin. He would spend much of the season in the middle of the pack or in the pit, sidelined by accidents and malfunctions, watching other drivers rack up points. The 2007 NASCAR season would provide a strong test of his fighting spirit, competitive fire, and good humor.

Spinning Out

Hamlin started the season by finishing 28th in the Daytona 500. He is quoted on FedEx.com's post-race report as saying: "We didn't finish where we wanted to today, but it certainly was not from a lack of effort. The crew did a great job on pit road today, and they continually earned us positions with great stops, but we just couldn't catch a break." It was a diplomatic

Hamlin crosses the finish line just ahead of Jeff Gordon to win the 2007 NASCAR Nextel Cup Series' Lenox Industrial Tools 300 in Loudon, New Hampshire.

way to talk about a disappointing race. It's important for professional athletes to be good sports, and that often means putting a positive spin on disappointing results and giving proper credit to your support staff.

Things looked up at the New Hampshire International Speedway, where Hamlin won his third career Cup race at the Lenox Industrial Tools 300 and found himself sixth in line in the Chase for the Cup, only 50 points behind the leader.

Yet, it turned out to be only a short break from a persistent spell of bad luck. During the Chase for the Cup, Hamlin had some setbacks, including a crash with Kyle Petty that ruined his chances for victory. He was disappointed and entered something of a tailspin. Later that season, at Homestead Miami Speedway, he finished 12th in the points standings, 580 points behind the leader.

While Hamlin had faced disappointment before, the 2007 racing season was really the first challenge to his golden-boy reputation. People still believed in him, and he continued to believe in himself, but it was a challenging year, one in which it was hard to keep his spirits up.

The Slump Deepens

The next year, 2008, started off no better at the Toyota Shootout debut. Hamlin's car was pushed into a wall at high speed. He and his car were OK and continued to race, but he couldn't quite get his groove back. He finished the race in ninth place. It was a disappointing finish but not disappointing enough to keep him out of the game.

The Daytona 500 was also a little disappointing. After leading 32 laps, Hamlin's car was damaged during a pit stop. He was somehow able to still finish in a very respectable 17th place, but it had looked like he had a great shot of winning the race before the accident.

He described the Daytona 500 to FedEx.com: "It wasn't the way we wanted this night or this race to end for the FedEx team. We were really good from the start, but, after that contact with the #43 on pit road, we were just never the same . . . The damage took a toll on our handling, and we just couldn't get it back. . . . The guys worked really hard and because of that we finished in the top 20."

At his next race, a damp, rain-slicked racetrack at the California Speedway kept Hamlin in a slight funk. Fifteen laps into the race, he hit a slick spot and went right into an outside wall. The rain caused another, bigger crash shortly thereafter. Hamlin finished the race in 41st place. It's easy to see how he might have felt a little down in the dumps, especially as he got off to such a fast and successful start early in his career. But he doesn't give up easily. There's always another race, and for Hamlin, the next one was at the Las Vegas Motor Speedway.

Lady Luck was with him in Vegas! Finally, a race where he could really show his stuff and start to get his groove back. A top ten finish at the United Auto Worker's (UAW) Dodge 400 got him back on track and feeling good.

The next race for Hamlin was the Kobalt Tools 500 at the Atlanta Motor Speedway. Technical problems, including the eventual loss of power steering, held him back. All things considered, he was lucky to make a top 20 finish. Although he had higher hopes for the race, he accepted the results of the day, graciously telling FedEx.com, "It was tough going out there today . . . I hate that a mechanical issue took away what could have been a good finish for this team, but we'll take a top 15 and look ahead to Bristol."

Bristol brought another bout of mechanical challenges and malfunctions. Loss of fuel pickup caused Hamlin to lose the lead and finish sixth, when he could've finished higher. Based on the evidence of his statements to his sponsor's online post-game report, it's apparent that the slump was starting to get to him: "It was another really frustrating day for us. I know I could have held those guys off there at the end, but we were either out of fuel or it was a fuel pickup problem like we had here last year . . . It's been that kind of season for us."

Back on Track

Hamlin was worried at his next race in Martinsville, Virginia. It was cold out, and his car wasn't handling as well as it might in more moderate temperatures. The race featured 20 lead changes split between eight drivers. But Hamlin was lucky and led when it counted. He took the lead on lap 427 of the 500-lap event and scored a much-needed win. He was thrilled, judging by his comments on FedEx.com: "This whole FedEx team did a fantastic job getting me off pit road when it counted. We got it all together finally."

Hamlin had regained his winning spirit. But would it last? It was looking good at the Samsung 500 at Texas Motor Speedway. He finished in the top five and moved up a few notches toward the Chase for the Cup. Also, in April he scored points-rich third-place finishes at both the Subway Fresh Fit 500 in Phoenix, Arizona, and Aaron's 499 at the Talladega Speedway in Alabama. By the end of April 2008, Hamlin was only 99 points behind the Sprint Cup series leader. Given that a single win could earn him 185 points, Hamlin's 2008 season was shaping up to be highly competitive. He was in the thick of the race for the Sprint Cup. As of early June, Hamlin was in fifth place in the Sprint Cup standings and well on his way to entering the Chase for the Cup. Want to see where the story goes from here? Visit FedEx Racing's Web site (http://www.fedex.com/us/sports/fedexracing).

CHAPTER 5

Paying It Forward

Even though he has become a popular and successful NASCAR driver, Denny Hamlin continues to be very involved with his family. His parents and grand-parents supported him in his early career and are still a big part of it today. He currently lives in Davidson, North Carolina, in the heart of NASCAR country.

As you might suspect, the main focus of Hamlin's life is racing. Even his downtime is spent thinking about racing. Word has it that he spends a lot of time playing computer racing games online. It's fun and probably helps keep his strategy, reflexes, and skills sharp.

The Denny Hamlin Foundation

It's not all fun and games, though, for Hamlin. He is using his fame and resources to really make a difference

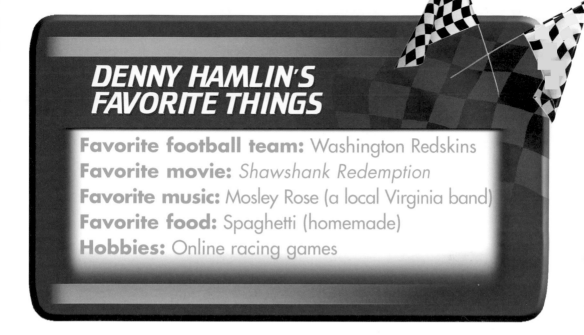

in people's lives through some creative charitable and fund-raising efforts.

Hamlin has a strong interest in helping children with serious diseases. In order to do this, he has formed his own nonprofit organization, the Denny Hamlin Foundation. Hamlin's official Web site (www.dennyhamlin.com) states that this nonprofit focuses on helping those with cystic fibrosis, an inherited disease that affects the lungs and digestive systems of 30,000 Americans and 70,000 people worldwide. The foundation makes grants to deserving recipients. It also works with more established charity organizations like the March of Dimes and the Cystic Fibrosis Foundation to raise funds to support sick children and their families and conduct research that may lead to a cure.

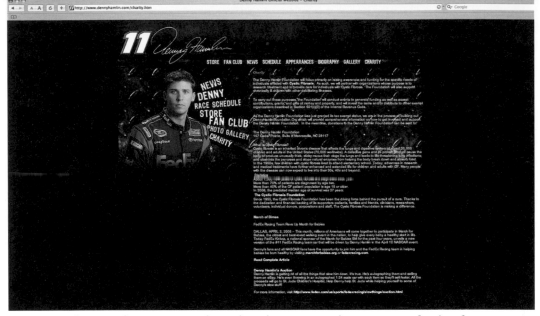

Hamlin's Web site (www.dennyhamlin.com) makes it easier for his fans to get the latest news and information about their favorite driver.

Hamlin's celebrity makes it easier for the causes he supports to get attention from the media and the many NASCAR fans who follow his career. This exposure, in turn, helps raise money for cystic fibrosis research and family and medical services for those affected by the disease. People who want to help him in this effort can make donations to his foundation, the March of Dimes, and/or the Cystic Fibrosis Foundation.

Visiting Hospitals

According to the FedEx Web site, Hamlin makes a point of visiting children's hospitals. He is also a major supporter of St. Jude's Children's Hospital, a leading treatment and research center for childhood cancers and other serious childhood illnesses.

Hamlin knows that a big part of getting well is feeling good. It's hard for sick kids to feel good. They have worries, take lots of medication, and feel very ill and weak

Giving back is important to Denny Hamlin. Here, he signs autographs for his fans at Children's Hospital in Los Angeles, California. He also donated a check for $25,000 to the hospital.

sometimes. Getting a chance to meet a famous NASCAR racer—and maybe even try on his helmet—can give kids a huge boost. It can lift their spirits and help them get better faster. Surely, it strengthens Hamlin's winning attitude, too.

What's Next for Denny Hamlin?

It's a safe bet that Denny Hamlin will continue his charity work. What's less certain is where his racing career will go from here. He's got a stellar record, especially for a still-young driver. And he's hit enough bumps in the road to have gained some real wisdom and experience.

Still, Hamlin's career goals are pretty straightforward. SI.com, the online partner to *Sports Illustrated* magazine, summarized his goals this way in an April 2008 post: "Not satisfied with being the Rookie of the Year in 2006 or with making the Chase for the Championship two years running, Hamlin is impatient to succeed." It quotes him as saying, "I'm competitive at everything I do, but it's hard to go out here and know that you have race-winning cars and not come home with a win."

Mark Ashenfelter, of ESPN.com, quotes Hamlin as saying, "A goal of my career is to be top five in points every single year. I don't want to be out of it." When his luck is down, he may adjust this goal a bit, but he always keeps his eye on the prize. And what is Denny Hamlin's larger goal? Always being in the thick of the race and winning it all.

Glossary

chassis A car's floorboard, interior, and roll cage. Essentially, the skeleton of a car.

Craftsman Truck Series NASCAR's modified truck racing series. It was launched in 1995.

DNF (Did Not Finish) When a driver does not finish a race, usually due to a crash or equipment malfunction.

mini stock car A smaller and less powerful stock car.

Nationwide Series NASCAR's second-highest level of stock car racing. Nationwide cars are similar to, but less powerful than, the cars raced at NASCAR's top level. The Nationwide Series is named after its sponsor. In past years, it has been named the Busch Series (2004–2007), the Busch Grand National Series (1984–2003), and the Budweiser Late Model Sportsman Series (1982–1983).

pit road The area where pit crews fix and fuel cars.

pole position First and most desirable starting position on the inside of the track, usually awarded to the fastest qualifying driver.

sponsor A person or company that financially supports a driver by paying his or her salary, travel, and all equipment costs. The sponsor's logo is generally on the driver's car. Denny Hamlin's sponsor is FedEx.

Sprint Cup NASCAR's top level of competition, in which America's best stock car racers compete. The series is named after its sponsor, Sprint. It has also been called the Nextel Cup (2004–2007) and the Winston Cup (1972–2003).

stock car A standard-make automobile (the kind average citizens drive) that has been modified for racing. Current eligible models include the Ford Fusion, Dodge Charger, Chevrolet Monte Carlo, and Toyota Camry.

stock car racing A blanket term for automobile racing. These races are generally held largely on oval rings of between approximately a quarter-mile (402 m) and 2.66 miles (4.28 km) in length or on road courses.

Victory Lane The "winner's circle." The area inside the oval of a racetrack where the winner parks and celebrates a win.

For More Information

Daytona International Speedway
1801 West International Speedway Boulevard
Daytona Beach, FL 32114
(386) 254-2700
Web site: http://www.daytonainternationalspeedway.com
Daytona International Speedway is the home of "the Great American
    Race"—the Daytona 500, the season-opening NASCAR Sprint
    Cup event. The enormous 480-acre (194 hectares) motorsports
    complex boasts the most diverse schedule of racing on the globe,
    thus earning it the title of "World Center of Racing."

The Denny Hamlin Foundation
157 Cedar Pointe, Suite A
Mooresville, NC 28117
This foundation is devoted to fund-raising efforts and grant disbursements
    on behalf of cystic fibrosis research and patient care.

DH Racing, Inc.
P.O. Box 2590
Davidson, NC 28036
(704) 896-8119
Web site: http://www.dennyhamlin.com
This is the official Denny Hamlin Web site and site for his fan club.

Joe Gibbs Racing
13415 Reese Boulevard West
Huntersville, NC 28078
(704) 944-5000
Web site: http://www.joegibbsracing.com
Former Super Bowl–winning head coach of the Washington Redskins,
    Joe Gibbs became a NASCAR team owner in 1991 and, with the
    help of his drivers and pit crews, has earned three NASCAR
    championships to match his three Super Bowl rings.

For More Information

National Association for Stock Car Auto Racing (NASCAR)
P.O. Box 2875
Daytona Beach, FL 32120
(386) 253-0611
Web site: http://www.nascar.com
NASCAR, which celebrated 60 years in 2008, is the sanctioning body
for one of North America's premier sports. NASCAR is the number
one spectator sport in the United States. It consists of three national
series (the NASCAR Sprint Cup Series, NASCAR Nationwide Series,
and NASCAR Craftsman Truck Series), four regional series, and
one local grassroots series, as well as two international series.
NASCAR sanctions more than 1,200 races at 100 tracks in more
than 30 U.S. states, Canada, and Mexico.

World Karting Association (WKA)
6051 Victory Lane
Concord, NC 28027
(704) 455-1606
Web site: http://www.worldkarting.com
The World Karting Association was formed in 1971 to regulate and
promote the sport of competitive kart racing. It establishes the rules
and procedures to set standards by which to sanction tracks and
conduct annual championships for various types of karting.

Web Sites

Due to the changing nature of Internet links, Rosen Publishing has
developed an online list of Web sites related to the subject of this book.
This site is updated regularly. Please use this link to access this list:

http://www.rosenlinks.com/bw/deha

For Further Reading

Allison, Liz. *The Girl's Guide to NASCAR*. Nashville, TN: Center Street, 2006.

Barber, Phil. *From Finish to Start: A Week in the Life of a NASCAR Racing Team*. Maple Plain, MN: Tradition Books, 2004.

Buckley, James, Jr. *NASCAR*. New York, NY: Dorling Kindersley Children, 2005.

Lipsyte, Robert. *Yellow Flag*. New York, NY: HarperTeen, 2007.

Miller, Timothy, and Steve Milton. *NASCAR Now*. Buffalo, NY: Firefly Books, 2004.

Poole, David, and Jim McLaurin. *NASCAR Essential: Everything You Need to Know to Be a Real Fan!* Chicago, IL: Triumph Books, 2007.

Schaefer, A. R. *The History of NASCAR*. Mankato, MN: Capstone Press, 2005.

Stewart, Mark, and Mike Kennedy. *NASCAR at the Track*. Minneapolis, MN: Lerner Publishing Group, 2008.

Stewart, Mark, and Mike Kennedy. *NASCAR in the Driver's Seat*. Minneapolis, MN: Lerner Publishing Group, 2008.

Woods, Bob. *Earning a Ride: How to Become a NASCAR Driver*. Chanhassen, MN: Child's World, 2003.

Bibliography

Ashenfelter, Mark. "Slow Start in Chase Puts Hamlin in Spoiler Role." ESPN.com, October 11, 2007. Retrieved April 2008 (http://sports. espn.go.com/rpm/news/story?series=2&id=3057503).

Associated Press. "Hamlin Foils Burton's Strategy to Win at Martinsville." ESPN.com, March 3, 2008. Retrieved April 2008 (http://sports. espn.go.com/espn/wire?section=auto&id=3320990).

Associated Press. "Moody Hamlin Happy After Martinsville Win: Moody Driver Looks to Carry Momentum into Texas." SportsIllustrated.com, April 2, 2008. Retrieved April 2008 (http://sportsillustrated.cnn. com/2008/racing/04/02/hamlin.ap/index.html).

FedExRacing. "Denny's Hamlin's Auction." Retrieved April 2008 (http:// www.fedex.com/us/sports/fedexracing/slowThings/auction.html).

FedExRacing. "Early Exit Caps Long Weekend for #11 Team." February 24, 2008. Retrieved April 2008 (http://www.fedex.com/ us/sports/fedexracing/race3-2008-post.html).

FedExRacing. "Hamlin, FedEx Racing Capture First Win of Season at Martinsville." March 30, 2008. Retrieved April 2008 (http:// www.fedex.com/us/sports/fedexracing/race7-2008-post.html).

FedExRacing. "Hamlin, FedEx Racing Hang On for 17th Place Finish at Daytona." February 17, 2008. Retrieved April 2008 (http:// www.fedex.com/us/sports/fedexracing/race2-2008-post.html).

FedExRacing. "Hamlin, FedEx Racing Ninth in Toyota Shootout Debut." February 9, 2008. Retrieved April 2008 (http://www.fedex.com/ us/sports/fedexracing/race1-2008-post.html).

FedExRacing. "Hamlin, FedEx Racing Score First Top-Ten of the Season at Las Vegas." March 2, 2008. Retrieved April 2008 (http:// www.fedex.com/us/sports/fedexracing/race3-2008-post.html).

FedExRacing. "Hamlin Wheels FedEx Ground Toyota to Fifth Place Finish in Samsung 500." April 6, 2008. Retrieved April 2008 (http:// www.fedex.com/us/sports/fedexracing/race8-2008-post.html).

FedExRacing. "Late Race Fuel Pickup Issue Sees Hamlin Lose Lead and Finish Sixth." March 16, 2008. Retrieved April 2008 (http:// www.fedex.com/us/sports/fedexracing/race6-2008-post.html).

FedExRacing. "Powered Down: Hamlin FedEx Racing 15th at Atlanta."
     March 9, 2008. Retrieved April 2008 (http://www.fedex.com/us/
     sports/fedexracing/race5-2008-post.html).

Martin, Mark, and Beth Tuschak. *NASCAR for Dummies*. Boston, MA:
     IDG Books, 2000.

Mitchell, Jason. "The Real Deal: NASCAR Driver Denny Hamlin Shows
     His Talent." StockCarRacing.com. Retrieved April 2008 (http://
     www.stockcarracing.com/thehistoryof/bio/scrp_0607_denny_
     hamlin_biography/index.html).

Murphey, Kerry. "Hamlin Has Off Track Injury." The Final Lap, April 30,
     2006. Retrieved April 2008 (http://www.finallapradio.com/
     newsarchives/news-archive-30-4-2006.shtml).

Newton, David. "Family, Friends Knew Hamlin Would Be a Star."
     NASCAR.com, November 10, 2006. Retrieved April 2008
     (http://64.233.167.104/search?q=cache:UYdm72qw1s0J:
     www.deanmotorsports.com/allnews.php%3FNewsID%3D82+
     dean+motosports+denny+hamlin&hl=en&ct=clnk&cd=1&gl=us&
     client=safari).

Rodman, Dave. "Hamlin All Positive About Toyota, COT, 'New' JGR."
     NASCAR.com, January 28, 2008. Retrieved April 2008 (http://
     www.nascar.com/2008/news/headlines/cup/01/28/dhamlin.
     kbusch.tstewart.toyota.cot/index.html).

Sports Illustrated. *Full Throttle: From Daytona to Darlington*. New York,
     NY: Sports Illustrated Books, 2004.

Index

B

Burton, Jeff, 4
Busch Series, 20, 23, 24

C

chassis, 10, 14
Clark, Thelma, 9, 15

D

Dean Motorsports, 18–19, 22
Denny Hamlin Foundation, 37
Did Not Finishes (DNFs), 6

E

Earnhardt Jr., Dale, 27
ESPN, 40

F

FedEx, 23, 30, 33, 34, 35, 38

G

Gillin, Chris "Spider," 27
go-karting, 8–14

H

Hamlin, Dennis, 16
Hamlin, Denny
  in the big leagues, 24, 26–29
  career slump, 30, 32–35
  and charity work, 36–40
  growing-up years, 8–16
  and #11 car, 4–6, 23, 29
  pro racing start, 17–23
  reputation, 26, 32
  sponsorship of, 17–19, 22, 23,
    30, 33–35, 38
Hamlin, Mary Lou, 16

J

Joe Gibbs Racing, 22

N

NASCAR rulebook, 19–21
National Kart News, 12
Nextel Cup Series, 20, 23, 24, 29

P

Petty, Kyle, 32
pole position, 6, 17, 19, 24,
  27, 29

R

restrictor plate, 24
rookie, 23, 24, 29

S

soapbox derby, 10
Sports Illustrated, 40
Sprint Cup, 4, 6, 20, 21, 23,
  32, 35
Stock Car Racing, 11

W

Winston Cup, 15

About the Author

Sarah Sawyer is a lifestyle and culture writer based in Minneapolis, Minnesota. Having been introduced to NASCAR by some fantastic neighbors, she is thrilled to have a chance to introduce her readers to Denny Hamlin.

Photo Credits

Cover, p. 18 Jason Smith/Getty Images for NASCAR; pp. 1, 4, 8, 17, 24, 30, 36 (silhouetted car) Rusty Jarrett/Getty Images for NASCAR; p. 5 Chris McGrath/Getty Images; pp. 9, 11 © AP Images; p. 23 Todd Warshaw/Getty Images for NASCAR; p. 25 Chris Graythen/Getty Images for NASCAR; p. 28 Ezra Shaw/Getty Images; p. 31 Matthew Stockman/ Getty Images; p. 39 Bob Riha/WireImage.

Designer: Evelyn Horovicz; Photo Researcher: Cindy Reiman